I0171582

The Laboratory of Time

and other cutup poems

by Peter Wortsman

BAMBOO DART PRESS

LOS ANGELES † NEW YORK † LONDON † MELBOURNE

The Laboratory of Time by Peter Wortsman

978-1-962316-05-7   Paperback

978-1-962316-06-4   Ebook

Cover photograph by Peter Wortsman

Layout and design by Peter Wortsman and Mark Givens

For information:

Bamboo Dart Press

chapbooks@bamboodartpress.com

Bamboo Dart Press 051

Pelekinesis

www.pelekinesis.com

BAMBOO DART PRESS

www.bamboodartpress.com

SHRIMPER

www.shrimperrecords.com

"Time will heal the hurt of it,
But time is a slow, old doctor,
Makin' his rounds
From town to town,
Black bag of death in his hand."

Peter Wortsman

Contents

I

The True Glue

II
The Five Books

Still Playing with Words
An Impromptu Prologue

Words belong to no one. They are all robbed, or borrowed if you prefer, from the babble of our contemporaries and the bibles of our forebears, who don't and didn't own them to begin with, but overheard or transcribed them from idle banter, news reports, and the chant of itinerant bards. Exhalations burdened with meaning, they are forever being uttered, stuttered and forgotten, trashed and mulched to fertilize new formulations.

What else is a cutup poem after all, or any kind of poem for that matter, but a wild flower sprouting out of the dirt! Rather than holding to traditional norms of prosody, the line in the transcription breaks more or less in conformance with the arrangement of the scattered snippets of type, permitting the words to dance on the page.

Though I have played with language for much of my life, cutup poetry remains for me a fresh terrain. Unlike the monotonously ticking kitchen clock that divides the day into temporal segments, each of the same duration, *The Laboratory of Time*, my third collection of experiments in the form, lets time be told in the way we live it, sometimes stretching a second into seeming eternity, sometimes compressing eternity into a second.

The first part, titled "The True Glue," comprises recycled

assemblages of words cut out of the newspaper that make a newfangled poetic sense.

The second part, titled "The Five Books," is an admittedly unorthodox retelling of biblical narrative. Out of respect for my ancestors, I decided not to cut up the ancient source still held sacred by some, but to extract the poetic sap and zap of it by means of a vertical transcription.

For those who may balk at this admittedly rather irregular mode of exegesis from top to bottom, I make no claim to originality, and would be willing to bet some mad Kabbalist beat me to it centuries ago. What fundamentalists hold to be holy writ is, in fact, a loose, rather imprecise retelling in a modern tongue, read from left to right, of a narrative originally told in an ancient tongue, read from right to left, and as such, necessarily, a distortion.

In the spirit of Zen, I gladly remain a rank beginner in my craft, glue splotches, ink spots, crooked type and all, rollicking in these messy assemblages like a boy of five tramping through a heap of fallen leaves or across a field of freshly fallen snow.

Peter Wortsman
October 14, 2024

I

The True Glue

the true
glue

"As a dog returneth to its vomit, so a fool returneth to his folly"

to parse truth from lie

I

cut text

AUGUST 18, 2023

The True Glue

"As a dog returneth to its
vomit, so a fool returneth to his
folly."
To parse truth from lie,
I
cut text.

August 18, 2023

ink on paper

Tinkering with

ink

just a few
black calligraphic marks floating across

a stained brown notebook.

Words took shape,

to ward off

the nameless,

lament

I do what I'm used to doing

"I couldn't do what a doctor or
lawyer does,"

But they couldn't do what I do.

find-
ing things — or letting things find

Me

break "all the rules

"I want it all, I want it now,

NOVEMBER 1, 2023

Ink on Paper

Tinkering with
ink,
just a few
black calligraphic marks floating across
a stained brown notebook,
words took shape
to ward off
the nameless
lament.
I do what I'm used to doing.
I couldn't do what a doctor or
lawyer does.
But they couldn't do what I do:
find-
-ing things – or letting things find
me.
Break all the rules!
I want it all, I want it now.

November 1, 2023

HOW TO WRITE A POEM

to think of it, makes it

cringe

to
intend to

is

to

kill.

language.
is unwelcoming

to

the

predictable,

cast nets and extend

artful
desire

become:

a mirror .

wrestling with the
raw

NOVEMBER 19, 2023

How to Write a Poem

To think of it, makes it
cringe;
to
intend to
is
to
kill;
language
is unwelcoming
to
the
predictable.

Cast nets and extend
artful
desire.

Become
a mirror,
wrestling with the
raw.

November 19, 2023

word painting

art

stutters

tight-lipped

overlaid with

ambiguous, multilayered

oddities

life may fling at

you

— even the bad things

distill

the

sublime.

SEPTEMBER 10, 2023

Word Painting

Art
stutters
tight-lipped
overlaid with
ambiguous, multilayered
oddities
life may fling at
you
–even the bad things
distill
the sublime.

September 10, 2023

found objects.

Every object tells a story.

in fossilized form,

d a wit-
ness to time and a guardian of memory.

SEPTEMBER 18, 2023

Found Objects

Every object tells a story
in fossilized form,
a wit-
ness to time and a guardian of memory.

September 18, 2023

found poetry

that
disarmed
word

compulsively ti
unnerving,

Mirrors,
and traps.

excitedly,
midstride,
yet distinct

in noise,
in stillness.

nothing there.

NOVEMBER 2, 2023

Found Poetry

That
disarmed
word,

compulsively
unnerving,

mirrors
and traps,

excitedly
midstride
yet distinct,

in noise,
in stillness,

nothing there.

November 2, 2023

Close Listening

Sit still.
Be quiet

taking in stimuli

like a shot of whiskey

Things
people

missteps and false starts;

the sickness
under the surface

prone to inertia,

I am a connoisseur of

distress

AUGUST 14, 2023

Close Listening

Sit still!
Be quiet!

Taking in stimuli
like a shot of whiskey:

things,
people,

missteps and false starts,

the sickness
under the surface.

Prone to inertia,
I am a connoisseur of
distress.

August 14, 2023

the world
beyond a book.

words

don't stay put in books,

bottled up

They

take

a deep dive

through a linguistic trapdoor.

an avalanche of

disembodied voices,

the nozzle cannot be turned off.

SEPTEMBER 17, 2023

The World Beyond a Book

Words
      don't stay put in books,
            bottled up,
they
take
   a deep dive
through a linguistic trapdoor,
   an avalanche of
         disembodied voices,
                  the nozzle cannot be turned off.

September 17, 2023

A
sketch
inspired by
water

imprint of
the wave

like
swirls of vivid
stillness,

Like vanishing rainfall,

fumbling for words.

I cannot sleep,

OCTOBER 3, 2023

A Sketch Inspired by Water

Imprint of
the wave,

like
swirls of vivid
stillness,
like vanishing rainfall —
fumbling for words,
I cannot sleep.

October 3, 2023

Beauty

What's that?

like
water

that seeps

from

rain-soaked

rocks

like

a line of sunlight

that slowly steals

along

stone walls,

like

wind over the earth,

with
bird's wings,
lift ed

in flight.

DECEMBER 8, 2023

Beauty – What's That?

Like
    water
        that seeps
            from
                rain-soaked
                    rocks...

Like a line of sunlight
    that slowly steals
        along
            stone walls...

Like wind over the earth
    with
        bird's wings
        lifted
            in flight...

December 8, 2023

Nature Morte

dirt, roots and insects hidden in the

grass

butterflies

in

the folds of a flower

fields.

of

com-

bustible dust

the

smell of death,

"If you want a true nature reserve, you
can't let humans in,"

SEPTEMBER 11, 2023

Nature Morte

Dirt, roots and insects hidden in the
grass,
butterflies
in
the folds of a flower,
fields
of
com-
-bustible dust,
the
smell of death...
"If you want a true nature reserve, you
can't let humans in."

September 11, 2023

slaughtering
Can this be art?'

I
won't

Refuse

narrative structure.

in the life span of a pig, from birth to
the slaughterhouse.

or

tease out

the ability of baboons to perceive
geometric shapes.

each sperm cell contained
within it a folded-up sheep embryo waiting
patiently to unfurl.

even bacteria are
unique.

But this narrative breaks down

in

the

messy

mise-en-scène

of

Roughly 200 people on death
row in Texas today,

Slaughtering – Can This Be Art?

I
won't
refuse
narrative structure
in the life span of a pig, from birth to
the slaughterhouse,
or
tease out
the ability of baboons to perceive
geometric shapes.

Each sperm cell contained
within it a folded-up sheep embryo waiting
patiently to unfurl.
Even bacteria are unique.

But this narrative breaks down
in
the
messy
mis-en-scène
of
roughly 200 people on death
row in Texas today.

September 13, 2023

doing
something that closely resembles nothing.

recycling

the deep,
unsaid.

scavenged from the city streets —

broken glass from car windshields

parking lot

tender
cathedral.

deliver
ma

unrepentant

I have no prayers to recite.

SEPTEMBER 18, 2023

Doing Something That Closely Resembles Nothing

Recycling

the deep
unsaid

scavenged from the city streets –
broken glass from car windshields,
parking lot,
tender
cathedral,

deliver
me
unrepentant.

I have no prayers to recite.

September 18, 2023

a durable fable

for

Henry David Thoreau.

Much ink has been spilled

foretelling what soon will come.

But,

Here's the thing that haunts me

Humans have never belonged

to the select society of the everlasting.

What

will I be when my body

is no longer ?

a virus. on ice,

an enormous spider

a
cricket creaking

'All I want

is

to

be

nothing at all.

'a

memory lapse.

under the shade of a tree

SEPTEMBER 25, 2023

A Durable Fable for Henry David Thoreau

Much ink has been spilled
foretelling what soon will come.
But
here's the thing that haunts me.
Humans have never belonged
to the select society of the everlasting.
What
will I be when my body
is no longer?
A virus on ice,
an enormous spider,
a
cricket creaking?
All I want
is
to
be
nothing at all,
a
memory lapse
under the shade of a tree.

September 25, 2023

for ro

the inti·mate lens

this beautiful loop between looking,
and being

a ruthless eye

erodes

protection

speaking by
dream·

time is but one of its beats.

to see the dead

"You
need to be the one that finishes the dream;"

SEPTEMBER 12, 2023

For R.O.

The intimate lens,

this beautiful loop between looking

and being,

a ruthless eye

erodes

protection.

Speaking by

dream,

time is but one of its beats.

To see the dead,

you

need to be the one that finishes the dream.

September 12, 2023

the parable of the
perfect walk

a runner on the
path to a particular destination

will always find

the
one thing you want to finally have
that points you to
where you want to go."

the

road behind everything that's in front of you.

"It's the whole idea of
walking around,

"I barely rest,"

mortal as I
am, I can, if need be, spend a whole day

entangled.

in

dismembered

memories

SEPTEMBER 27, 2023

The Parable of the Perfect Walk

A runner on the
path to a particular destination
will always find
the
one thing you want to finally have
that points you to
where you want to go:
the
road behind everything that's in front of you.
It's the whole idea of
walking around.
I barely rest,
mortal as I
am, I can, if need be, spend a whole day
entangled
in dismembered
memories.

September 27, 2023

nocturnal sensuality

bodies at night.

blunt cravings

the pleasant hum of human voices.

somehow
lush

Trees are
quarreling with one another.

a screamer.

yowls, glottals, keening long lines, baby
cries, witchy cackles —

"Yesssss!"

"Nooooo!"

"What the hell is that?"

It's like a hymn.

adroitly filtered

The half-life of grief

performed by

a gospel choir.

AUGUST 18, 2023

Nocturnal Sensibility

Bodies at night,
blunt cravings,
the pleasant hum of human voices
somehow
lush ...
Trees are
quarreling with one another.
A screamer
yowls, glottals, keeping long lines, baby
cries, witchy cackles –
"Yesssss!"
"Nooooo!"
"What the hell is that?"
It's like a hymn
adroitly filtered,
the half-life of grief
performed by
a gospel choir.

August 18, 2023

staring at the sky.

We all have this idea of what space is sup-
posed to be like.

boundary between earth and sky,

the murky zone

empty, and still,

the contours of what would

wedged

between

Electric Dreams

holding back a
great and terrifying force.

SEPTEMBER 3, 2023

Staring at the Sky

We all have this idea of what space is sup-
posed to be like –
boundary between earth and sky,
the murky zone,
empty and still,
the contours of what would
wedged
between
electric dreams,
holding back a
great and terrifying force.

September 3, 2023

lavish
advertisement for

an angel
lamenting

Demon Nymph,

"porcelain" skin.
of.

obsession

We all have our dolls,

externalized de-

posits of

dream

and

dread

What is fantasy, if not the dancing silhou-
ette of some unspeakable

longing

playing
loud.?

OCTOBER 22, 2023

Lavish Advertisement for an Angel Lamenting

Demon nymph,
porcelain skin
of
obsession –
we all have our dolls,
externalized de-
posits of
dream
and
dread.
What is fantasy, if not the dancing silhou-
ette of some unspeakable
longing
playing
loud?

October 22, 2023

snatches of
remembrance.

Date

I've begun to amass
these vessels of memory.
amphoras,

weighty with time.

intense turmoil

in a tiny
intimacy

the monologue leans
foul-mouthed

a melding of

manic

and

still

— life is messy,

the membrane between

promise

and

pleasure

death

a desperate

metaphor

in doubt,

NOVEMBER 6 2023

Snatches of Remembrance

I've begun to amass
these vessels of memory,
amphoras
    weighty with time,
        intense turmoil
           in a tiny
             intimacy.

    The monologue leans
foul-mouthed,
      a melding of
        manic
         and
          still,
    the membrane between
      promise
        and
         pleasure,
—life is messy,
and death
    a desperate
      metaphor
        in doubt.

November 6, 2023

The laboratory of
time

This all may sound bleak, but

to go back

, with

an eerie and
persistent hum from the heavens

13.8 billion years back

to

The beginning of time

to articulate

the retina-teasing movement of

a single moment

the present-tense

and

.... less than one-trillionth
)f a second after the Big Bang.

how one moment transforms to become
another.

detectable now
only as a faint, omnipresent hiss

"The past is never dead."

pinched, squeezed

and dissected.

It can even

release

The presence of a future

SEPTEMBER 7, 2023

The Laboratory of Time

This all may sound bleak, but
to go back
with
an eerie and
persistent hum from the heavens,
13.8 billion years back
to
the beginning of time,
to articulate
the retina-teasing movement of
a single moment,
the present-tense
and
less than one trillionth
of a second after the Big Bang,
how one moment transforms to become
another,
detectable now
only as a faint, omnipresent hiss,
the past is never dead;
pinched, squeezed
and dissected,
it can even
release

the presence of a future.

September 7, 2023

speaking
through
desire

Date

Where are we?

Who is speaking?

not just a rendezvous with
a mirror

the whole creature

self,

soul, and

that thing

the nerve

thinking

dirty

thoughts,

with a nod to

the

forbidden

my body

is

shaking

But

I'm still

placing the last piece of the

puzzle

in

fertile

fantastical

interlocke

fields of

wild

OCTOBER 29, 2023

Speaking Through Desire

Where are we?
Who is speaking?
    Not just a rendezvous with
a mirror,

            the whole creature,
            self,
            soul and
            that thing,
            the nerve
            thinking
            dirty
            thoughts,
            with a nod to
            the
            forbidden.
            My body
            is
            shaking,
            but
            I'm still
            placing the last piece of the
            puzzle
            in
            fertile,
            fantastical
            interlocked
            fields of
            wild.

October 29, 2023

II

The Five Books

Transcribed, translated, extracted, thus thrice
removed from the primordial mouth, as myth would
have it, in words first muttered by a stuttering
prophet with rocks in his mouth to still the stammer,
these cut-up fragments capture telling nuggets.

Re-Genesis

In the beginning...

void
the deep

good
darkness
rules the divide

every creeping thing
subdue it

face
yielding seed
is life, I
meat

And on the seventh day...

every it
grew
nostrils
in Eden

the name
of the name
in the midst of knowledge

fruit serpent
beguiled
my bones
called
shall I hide
is anything too hard for
a son
denied

thy brother
am I
blood
driven
and name
begat
of
language
slime

him
man
the creeping thing

and beast
of I
clean beast
blessed

I have taken
wife

mouth
fountains

windows
upon
nights

two of all flesh
creeping
after
kind

then a mother of nations
fell upon his face
and laughed

dove
lo
plucked

they delivered
things
firstlings
fell

blood
surely

the wine
within

sons
tongues
nations
foreskin
[the same old refrain]

may
a name
see
thy seed
builded

make cakes
unto the herd

eat
thy wife?

where
to thee this night
escape consumed

shall this
kill me?

Exodust

Now these are the names...
of the loins

Behold

the river
alive
with slime
therein

behold
angel flame
I am hand
THAT I AM
this is my memorial

O anger
speak glad

the tale
shall not
idle

wife, she bore him
lay
forth
children

down his rod
morning—lo
finger of God

and the sea
I am
sea
hardened
I will sing

Behold
children
that we are
little
and stink

And it came to pass...

this thing
I do
the noise
of
it

open a pit
man
dig
the dowry of virgins
devouring eyes

in the coupling
another curtain
in the coupling
fifty loops
cunning flesh hooks
between the holy and
the veil

And it came to pass...

I will write
upon the morning
in my mother's milk

this thing
going out of it
into the midst of it

curious girdle
graven with names

This Remnant of Meat

And the Lord called
the herd

blemish: he shall
flay the sons

skin his head
the sin
is known

utter it
or
lips do evil

the lost thing
his
flesh
hath
on

be broken
be used

wring off its head
and give it
eternity

The Renowned Tribes
(a parable)

old and upward
stand

the renowned
tribes

all
were
children
[once]
names
in the wilderness
instruments
under
death
redeemed

both male and female
carnally
cursing

so it was

they journeyed
they rested in tents

And it came to pass...

a wind
called
dream
told them
this is the fruit of it

–Lo
this evil
me–

rod of
thy rods
salt
to thy seed

dip it
kindled
angel

make it good

no servile
trumpets
nest in rock

until your carcasses be
wasted in the wilderness
hang
on

Poor Upright Animal Aloof
(an epitaph)

tongue
O God
give
my groaning
angry
instruments

eyelids
be
my throne

who
is God
but a byword
for
death
forgotten

poor
upright
animal
aloof
forget God
remember
the seat of
delight

walk
death
like a dog on a leash
nostrils
honoring
dust
when I was
womb
belly
trouble
my tongue
a melted
sword upon thy thigh
we beat
the wind
and swallowed
imagined
children

but now
I am a groaning worm
water
my grief
tomorrow
thou art me

Acknowledgments

"The Five Books," a vertical rereading of the first five books of the Old Testament, also known as "The Five Books of Moses," first appeared in *Mungbeing Magazine*.

BAMBOO DART PRESS

112 N. Harvard Ave. #65
Claremont, CA 91711

chapbooks@bamboodartpress.com
www.bamboodartpress.com

www.ingramcontent.com/pod-product-compliance
Lightning Source LLC
Chambersburg PA
CBHW081643040426
42449CB00015B/3439